Published 2008 by Concordia Publishing House
3558 S. Jefferson Avenue, St. Louis, MO 63118-3968
1-800-325-3040 • www.cph.org

Text © 2008 Julie Stiegemeyer
Illustrations © 2008 by Concordia Publishing House

Manufactured in China.

1 2 3 4 5 6 7 8 9 10   17 16 15 14 13 12 11 10 09 08

A STORY OF CHRISTMAS

Fear Not, Joseph!

BY JULIE STIEGEMEYER   ILLUSTRATED BY CHERI BLADHOLM

CONCORDIA PUBLISHING HOUSE • SAINT LOUIS

The daylight faded in my carpenter's shop as I chiseled away at the wood to shape the plow. Wood chips flew through the air as I scratched across the rough surface. The plow had to be finished by morning; it was going to be a long night.

"Joseph," a voice from behind me called. I turned and there was Mary, my betrothed, my beloved, her eyes bright with smiles. "I have news," she said.

"Amazing news!"

I set my tools aside, glad for the moment's rest as Mary sat beside me on a bench.

"I can hardly believe it, Joseph. An angel has come to me!" She paused, looking down. "Joseph, he said I am to have a Son, the Son of the Most High God."

"An angel?" I interrupted.

Had I heard her correctly? "An angel came to you?"

"He said the Holy Spirit would come upon me, the power of God would overshadow me, and the child would be called holy—the Son of God."

I looked at Mary, my stomach twisting and my thoughts whirling. I wanted to trust her, but I did not believe her words. *An angel visited her? She was already with child? But we weren't even married yet!*

"Mary," I said, troubled. "Maybe you had a dream. Go home and sleep. We will talk tomorrow." I turned back to my work.

"But Joseph . . ." Mary said, with sadness in her voice.

"Tomorrow," I replied. I had to finish the plow—that much I knew to be true. So I tried to put Mary out of my mind.

The dull light of dawn seeped through my window when I finally lay down to rest. The plow was finished, but sleep would not come easily. My thoughts raced with Mary's words.

Who was the father of this child? I wondered. *I couldn't marry her now, could I? No. Things had changed too much. I'd have to tell her so tomorrow.*

At last I must have fallen sleep because I suddenly woke with words echoing in my dreams.

"Fear not, Joseph!"

An angel had come as I slept and spoke to me in my dreams. "Take Mary as your wife," he said, "for what is conceived in her is from the Holy Spirit. She will bear a Son, and you shall call His name Jesus, for He will save His people from their sins."

I shook away my sleepiness, quickly dressed, and rushed out into the morning bustle to Mary's house.

I saw her, sweeping. "Mary!" I wrapped her in my arms. "I will take care of you—and the child," I said, despite the questions still prickling at my thoughts.

"But you were so different last night, Joseph."

"You are not the only one who hears angels," I said, smiling at my beloved.

"We will call the child Jesus."

Months passed.

When we learned that the king demanded that we make a record of our family, Mary and I journeyed together to the home of my great-great-great-grandparents: Bethlehem. Mary, now my wife, would soon bear the child the angel promised.

Poor Mary. I could not afford anything more than a dirty donkey to carry her. So on we plodded through the crisp dusty days and the star-filled nights as the angel's words echoed in my thoughts.

"Fear not, Joseph!"

The crowds pressed in on us as we walked the streets of Bethlehem. All of these people, descended from King David. Amazing! Soon, however, what seemed amazing became a problem. From inn to inn we went, searching for a place to stay.

"Please!"

I begged an innkeeper. "My wife will soon give birth! Do you not have a little space for us?"

He shook his head. "There is no room."

Just then, a boy peeked out. "Father," he said, tugging at the innkeeper's sleeve. "Could they stay in the stable?"

"I suppose, Caleb," the innkeeper said gruffly. "Show them the way, but hurry back."

The boy went ahead of us with a small lamp. "This way," he pointed to the hillside behind the house and led us to a cave almost hidden behind a rocky crag. Inside there was shelter from the wind in the earthy dampness. The boy got out clean straw and laid it in an empty space. I helped Mary down to the straw.

"Joseph," she said, trembling and crying in pain. "The child is coming."

No, I thought. *Not now. Not here.*

I shuddered as the damp cold seeped into my skin, but then I remembered the angel's words.

"Fear not, Joseph!"

"God will care for you, Mary," I told her, trying not to shiver in the darkness. "Our Savior is coming."

The boy started to leave the stable. "Wait!" I rushed over to him. "Wait…."Caleb, my wife needs help. Could your mother or grandmother come?"

"I will ask," he said, and ran out.

I gathered some wood from
the corner of the stable and made
a small fire. I tried not to frighten
the animals as they shuffled uneasily.
I was glad of their company.
And their warmth.

Mary's cries were growing more desperate
when—finally—a woman peered into the stable.
She went to Mary. "My poor girl. Let me help you."
Mary nodded a greeting through her pain.
Her firstborn child would be born here in this cold
stable among strangers!

I wished it could be different.

The woman helped Mary while I gathered
water and more wood.

At last, the miracle came.

The cry in the
star-filled Bethlehem night.

The sigh of His mother.

The Baby cradled in my arms.

I wrapped the Child in Mary's veil, the only spare cloth we had. We had nothing—barely a shelter, no food, no wealth. Yet at that moment, in this tiny bundle, in this small, helpless Child, I found hope.

I knew that the angel's words were true.

God would save His people, as He had promised. Here was the King of Creation, with us, to save us, as the angel had said.

T ime passed.

We stayed in Bethlehem, settling into a little house. And then we heard again from the Lord's messenger. Angel words came to me in another dream. The Baby's life was in danger. We had to escape. I needed to protect the Child and His mother from the evil King Herod.

So, Mary and I walked out into the night, on toward Egypt, with Bethlehem at our backs. Like Abraham, our ancestor, we trusted that God's hand was leading us and His love supporting us, His promises swaddled in the Child I carried in my arms.

AUTHOR'S NOTE

Fear Not, Joseph is a story inspired by the accounts of Joseph in the Gospels, particularly from the books of Matthew and Luke. Many details come from the Bible itself. The Bible tells us that Joseph was a carpenter (Matthew 13:55) and that he intended to divorce Mary quietly (Matthew 1:19). But an angel came to him in a dream and revealed to him that Mary's Child was God Himself.

After Joseph's initial doubts, he did not hesitate. Following each biblical account of an angel giving Joseph a message, we read how quickly Joseph acted: "When Joseph woke from sleep, he did what the angel of the Lord commanded him" (Matthew 1:24); "And he rose and took the child" (Matthew 2:14). Joseph's unflinching devotion to his duty to protect the Christ Child is inspiring.

The human element of this drama is understated in the Scriptures; *Fear Not, Joseph* is an attempt to fill in the blanks of what the experience may have resembled for Joseph and his wife.

While writing this book, I gained a deeper appreciation for the quiet and yet necessary role Joseph played as guardian of our Lord Jesus. Jesus was not Joseph's natural son, but God made Joseph His adopted father, the provider and caretaker of Mary and our Savior, Jesus. God often chooses the humble and unassuming to be His hands and to share His mercy with others. Joseph was one such person.